support@blackseedspublishing.com
www.blackseedspublishing.com

Please note that all products and services offered by our company are strictly intended for educational and informational purposes. Your personal success in implementing the ideas or strategies presented in this book depends on various individual factors, including your health, skills, knowledge, abilities, dedication, goals, relationships, compassion for others, and financial circumstances, among others.

Since these factors differ among individuals, we cannot guarantee specific outcomes or results in any area of your life or endeavors. It is important to understand that we make no warranties or guarantees regarding the attainment of specific results from the information, programs, or services provided. Additionally, we do not provide any licensed or professional medical, legal, therapeutic, tax, or financial advice within our program. The information contained herein should not be considered a substitute for the expertise and services of trained professionals in their respective fields, including but not limited to medical, psychological, financial, or legal matters.

ISBN: 979-8-9878956-2-7

Printed in the United States

"You don't have to wait on a paycheck, you just have to have the courage NOT to. There is a difference between an idea and a profit PLAN!"

-Rev. Dr. Dawniel Winningham
Master Life & Business Coach

YOUR BOOK

From Idea to Empire

IS YOUR

Building a Brand You Can Bank

Brand

WRITTEN BY

JAMIE HOPKINS

CEO, BLACK SEEDS PUBLISHING & SERIAL ENTREPRENEUR

"I just want people to heal and I know one of the ways to do that: tell your story. As a healer, I know there are people hurting and it hurts me. I wish I could take the pain from the world, but I cannot. I can only share my gifts to heal one author, one reader, at a time."

- Jamie Hopkins, CEO Black Seeds Publishing

Table of Contents

Breaking Bad....................1

Write Your Way to the Top....................8

Find Your Niche and Own It....................12

From Ideas to Pages....................29

Launch Day....................42

Maximizing Your Book's Potential....................53

The Future is Bright....................73

Chapter and Verse....................78

Writing the Next Chapter....................82

The Power of Word of Mouth....................90

Client Management....................98

Leaving a Legacy....................103

Bottom Line....................110

About the Author....................113

Breaking Bad

I've always been different. I've always followed the beat to my own drum, even if it led me into despair and destruction. No matter what, I learned to trust my instincts, which in turn meant I had to trust *myself*.

After so many failed relationships, being dumped and abandoned, used and thrown away, you start to wonder about the trend of this long strand of bad luck!

It's only so far that you can blame the abusers or the perpetrators who victimized you. It's only heard and tolerated for so long by those around you. Yes, I said it, they "tolerate" you.

Your tantrums. Your quick temper. Your 'my way or the highway' attitude. Your constant nagging about absolutely everything. How does it feel to hear or to know that the people you hold dear to your heart, *tolerate* your existence?

That was me. Five years ago.

After another failed relationship and shun from the friend circle, I was found deserted. Alone. To look at *myself*.

Talk about a raw and dirty "come to Jesus" moment! It was the exact moment I decided to stop running and face my demons.... my fears head on.

ME.

I was my biggest demon. All of my fears, anxieties, depressions, suicide attempts, rapes, homelessness, sleeping in empty church parking lots, miscarriages, abortions... battle scars bae bae!!! All of that was inside this 130-pound frame.

My demons were killing me. My silence was killing me softly. I was a walking dis-ease.

Do you want to know why? Because I was running from the inevitable... my purpose.

I didn't like being a "healer." It came (comes) with too many scars.

Healers attract sick people!

And being untrained in my gift, I attracted the *wrong* sick people and allowed them to stick around longer than they were intended to.

I took in the sick puppies, loved them back to health, and they went back to their owner.

I was the one answering every call or text. I was the one soothing the fears and encouraging the good behaviors. I was the one fulfilling the nasty desires you would never speak out loud. I was your closet whore. And I loved you back to health.

Only to abandon me, then on to the next!

It became a cycle that I quickly got lost in. The whirlwind of failed relationship after failed relationship. The same story with the same ending.

Mundane. Pointless. Cyclical. And I couldn't get off this rollercoaster ride!

Until five years ago. I made a promise to my inner me that I was going to find her, and rescue her. If I died trying, the world will know my story, my truth. It took only five years to tell it right.

So my friend, my business partner, my fellow entrepreneur... we ALL have a story. This business saved my life and my family because it gave me **purpose outside of my pain, outside of my mistakes, outside of my poor judgement.** This business became my brand.

My brand is healing. That is ME.

You can take your story and build a brand for your business and your family, too. Your book IS your brand (and also your legacy, but we will get to that part later).

Keep reading.... let's talk about it.

Pssst... I'm a storyteller, so grab your cup of coffee, tea, favorite beverage, favorite snuggie, highlighter and pen - find a comfy spot, and let's get all up in my kool-aid!

The greatest example I can give you is mine own. Oh, honey and I got plenty!!

Entrepreneurial Hard Knock Lesson #1

"Don't be afraid to reinvent yourself. If one business idea doesn't work, make some changes and try something else. The key is to FIND the right recipe for YOU and how you want to live. And guess what... NO ONE can define that but YOU.. (sorry, not sorry)."

- Jamie Hopkins

Your Book Is Your Brand

The Power of a Book in Building Your Business

Write Your Way to the Top

Come on, friend! I don't have to tell you that books stand the test of time! You're reading one and, if this book does what the vision said it would do, you're reading this eons after it's been published!

You may even be holding an ancient, sacred text in your hands right now. And yes, I am well aware that the digital age is upon us, however, I will stand on this statement: printed books stand the test of time! They will never grow old or extinct, unlike my friends the West African Black Rhinoceros - they no longer exist. But books...

Books are the fabric of this earth. It tells the stories of the dead. It keeps the secrets of the land. People die, animals die, you and I will die someday... anything with life will eventually die. But not books.

📖

The funny thing is, it is the responsibility of the 'living' to write the books and keep the world moving and advancing forward.

Hence, my proposition of why this book is in your hands or on your device at this time... you're interested to hear and I'm eager to share!

📖

Your Book is your business journey. We all have one. As an entrepreneur, the journey starts with the business idea. And from that idea to opening the doors of operation, is the middle of your business journey.

Yeah, you probably thought I was going to say that the business idea was actually the start of your business journey. But it is not.

The start happened before you were manifested in the physical earth realm. It started when you were a thought in the Creator's mind. **You were created with purpose.** That is a fact. And keep reading... I'm going to prove it!

Nope, don't go grab your bibles... you won't need it for this journey or this story... I won't make it super spiritual, but please understand that your spirit is part of the "whole" you, and this book will address the whole you, in all of your glory - without having to spill all the beans like the author of this book. :-)

Your brand story, or book, will open doors for you and your bank account that you couldn't imagine. I'm just going to talk about a few of them, but please do your due diligence to research more!

What the Experts Say 🤓

Writing a book can be a great way to establish yourself as a go-to expert in your industry or niche! Not only does it showcase your knowledge and skills, but it also serves as a tangible way for people to learn about you and your business. Plus, it's a great way to stand out from the competition and attract new clients and opportunities.

And let's not forget, once your book is published, it can open up opportunities for media coverage and speaking engagements, which can give you even more visibility and reach!

All in all, writing a book can be a fun and rewarding way to build your brand and business.

So let's start with the basics first: Defining your brand.

Defining Your Brand with Your Book

Find Your Niche and Own It

In this chapter, we will dive into the importance of defining and owning your niche, and how it ties into your brand-building efforts through your book.

We will explore the key components of defining your niche and establishing your brand. By understanding your target audience and the problems they face, you can position yourself as a solution provider in your niche.

Defining your USP will set you apart from the competition and give you a clear message to communicate in your book and marketing efforts.

And establishing your brand voice and message will ensure consistency across all your marketing efforts and help you connect with your target audience.

By the end of this chapter, you will have a solid foundation for building your brand with your book.

Success Tip #1

"Get yourself a notebook designated just for your business ideas. For those who believe, pray over it and bless it - dedicate it back to the Universe and the Ancient Wise One. Surrender to your own thoughts that will make you rich."

- Black Seeds Publishing

Now that you've gotten your Business Wealth Creation Notebook (I made that name up, but you can call it what you want :) ... turn the page >>>

Understanding Your Niche

So, what is a niche? In layman's terms, a niche is a *specific group* of people who have a *common problem* or need that your *business can solve*. Think of it as a neighborhood where everyone has similar interests and needs.

Why is it important to find your niche? Well, imagine trying to sell ice cream in a town where everyone is lactose intolerant. It's going to be pretty hard to sell, right? That's why it's crucial to know who you're trying to sell to.

By focusing on a specific group of people, you'll have a better chance of connecting with them and building a strong brand that resonates with them.

Let's take the example of a nutritionist who wants to write a book and build a business. The first step is to identify their niche. They may start by realizing that they have a passion for helping people with autoimmune diseases.

This can become their niche, and they can position themselves as the go-to expert in this area.

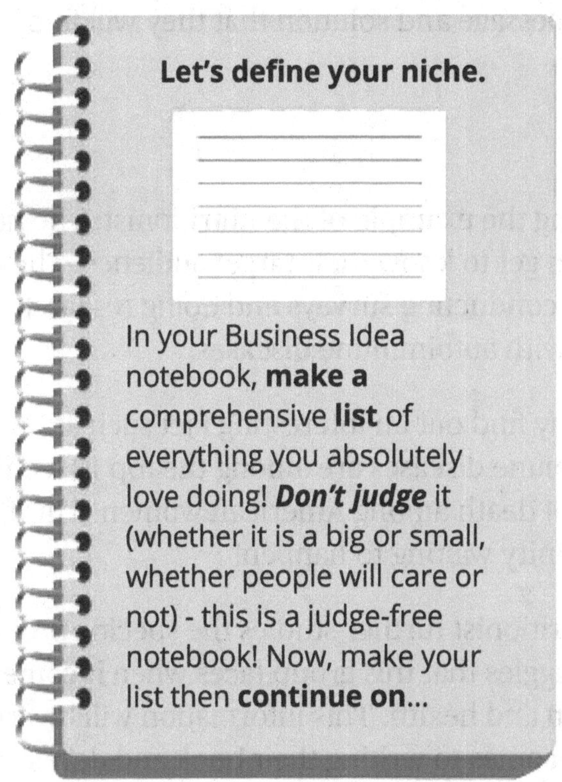

Once you have settled on your niche, the next step is to figure out who your target audience is. This is the group of people who you want to help with your book and business.

Get to know your target audience by understanding their problems and what they need. This will help you craft a message and solution that they will find valuable.

Following the example of the nutritionist: The next step is to get to know their target audience. They may start by conducting surveys and doing research on people with autoimmune diseases.

They may find out an interesting fact such as autoimmune diseases are among the top 10 leading causes of death among American women. This is an opportunity waiting to happen!

The nutritionist further studies the specific problems and struggles that this group faces when it comes to nutrition and health. This information will be crucial when it comes to writing their book and developing their business. They are speaking to one group versus everybody and their aunties.

When it comes to your niche, look at what's out there and see what other people are doing. There are tons of free information available on the internet, so take advantage and sharpen those research skills. There's a popular search engine that will assist you in your quest! **wink wink**

Consider...

What can you offer that's different and unique? This will help you identify opportunities in your niche and give you a *competitive edge*.

Now that they have a good understanding of their target audience, the nutritionist will do some research to see what's already out there. They'll look at books and websites on this topic, and see what other experts are saying. This will help them identify what makes their approach unique and what opportunities they have in this niche.

For example, they may realize that there's a gap in the market for a book that specifically addresses the needs of people with autoimmune diseases, using a whole-foods based approach. This realization can lead to a *unique selling proposition* (USP) for their brand, which will set them apart from the competition.

They can now use this information to write a compelling book and build a successful business.

Just like that.

So you may be asking, "It's as simple as that? If that is the case, everybody would be doing it!" And you may have a case, but hear my point...

There is nothing new under the sun. It's an old, ancient proverb that has filtered it's way through generations of time.

I know you would want to believe that your idea is unique and special and one-of-a-kind... until you see someone else doing it and suddenly feel "disappointed" that you "missed your turn".

I'm not quite sure where the ideology came from that only one person can do one thing or sell one product/ service... but we've seemed to have adopted that train of thought. Which in turn, limits our motivation to succeed in life on our own terms. We adopt the terms of life others wish for us, because we've been disappointed by a false ideology.

That competitive advantage I mentioned earlier is not about being the only one doing something, it's about adding your spirit to that thing and making it unique to you and your target audience.

Let me say this loudly: YOU are the secret sauce, boo!

It's your energy that you put into every part of your business. That's why it's important that you don't skip the first part: deciding what you love to do.

I'll talk more on this later, let's move on for now.

I hope this text reminds you that you are in control of your destiny.

Okay, enough mushy-emotiony-feelingy-stuff. Back to these money bags.

Your Unique Selling Proposition (USP) More Defined

Okay, so you've got a handle on your niche and your target audience, but what sets you apart from the competition? This is where your USP comes in.

Your USP is what makes you unique, what makes your book and brand stand out. It's what sets you apart and makes you the go-to expert in your field.

So, how do you figure out your USP? It starts with doing some research and introspection. You need to ask yourself what makes you special and what sets you apart from others in your field.

You can also look at your competitors and see what they're offering, and find a way to differentiate yourself.

For example, say that you are a graphic designer. Now, there are several different ways you can approach the graphic designer field, but if you're paying attention to current trends, you know that artificial intelligence is taking over the scene.

So in order to position yourself in an ever-changing environment, you assert your skills using artificial intelligence tools. You can call it "Convergence: When Creativity Meets AI". It's unique, it's trendy, and it's what's happening NOW.

Does that make sense?

Let's go back to my last case study about the nutritionist again:

After researching the market, they may realize that while many books on nutrition and autoimmune diseases exist, they all take a similar approach that focuses on cutting out certain foods.

However, the nutritionist has a different approach that focuses on using whole foods to help heal the gut and support the immune system. This becomes their USP.

By using a whole-foods based approach, the nutritionist differentiates themselves from the competition and becomes the go-to expert for people with autoimmune diseases who want to improve their health through food.

This sets the foundation for a strong brand and a successful business.

It's important to identify your USP early on, as it will be the foundation for your brand and will help you stand out in a crowded market.

Time To Practice!

Grab your business idea notebook again. This time, you want to start a "Research section" where you can keep track of your "aha" moments during your research phase.

Schedule time for research and development. This is your learning process phase, which will also increase your awareness, thus making manifestations easier. In other words, your book is being birthed and this is part of that birthing process :)

Next: make a list of your competitors that stood out to you the most. Your experience from start to finish as you connected with their brand.

Note how it made you feel.

THAT'S how you want your target audience to feel with your brand.

Now, next to each competitor's name, write down what you feel is missing from their brand.

At the end, tally up all of the "missing in their brands" into one page or one list.

Now, you're looking at a good list of USPs. Yours for the picking!

Simple as that! Told ya.

Establishing Your Brand Voice and Message

Once you've got your niche and USP figured out, it's time to work on your brand voice and message. This is how you'll communicate your unique approach and what sets you apart.

It's important to have a consistent voice and message that people can recognize and remember, so they'll come to you when they need help or advice.

Now, this is where some business coaches or other industry leaders may disagree, but what really burns my biscuits is those who try to do everything for everybody!

Those "Jack of All Trades and Master of None"...

Those "do anything for a buck" folks that also crowd the entrepreneurial workspace. Or worst, the ones who start a hobby, undercharging folks and throwing a monkey wrench in the entire ecosystem! With their overworked and underpaid mentality...

It's partly because of them, that you will have to prove yourself before you can even start your business!

And THAT'S where your book comes in. People will read your book first (without having to know you personally) before they will hire you.

In order to hire you, you have to damn near give up your first born child! Spend hours on the phone with them before they even make a decision to buy from you.. only for them to say they don't have the money. Whomp whomp!

Epic fail! 👎

"Preparation + Strategy = Success" - I don't know who said that, but that's what just came to my mind as I'm writing this very personal love letter to you. (Okay, not *love* love, but 'love' as in humanity 🩶 - to be very clear).

But I digress...

🪷

Your brand voice is how you speak and write about your niche and your approach. It's your unique tone and personality, and it should reflect who you are and what you stand for.

When developing your brand voice, think about your values, your personality, and what makes you unique. This will help you find your authentic voice and communicate your message in a way that resonates with your audience.

As I mentioned earlier, I am a healer. I am also a writer and a publisher. I don't even want to go into how much money I've spent on business coaches who couldn't "get my vision". How many countless hours, sweat, tears, dollars went into designing the perfect voice for me.

Many have tried to sway me from being a healer and mixing that with business. But listen, whether you buy my book or hire me to publish yours, if you come over here, healing is what it is. So why hide who I am because it makes others uncomfortable?

That's my unique selling point.

Oprah Winfrey was known for giving away huge prize gifts as part of her talk show. She was unique to that, even started a trend and others started to do the same - but never at the magnitude of Miss Oprah honey.

I am known for making people cry. :) I don't want to go into my legacy yet in here, I'll go more into this later.

But getting back to my unique selling point: I am a publisher who heals through the use of literary art.

Let's go back to our nutritionist. Their brand voice may be warm, supportive, and down-to-earth. They may use a conversational tone and humor to make their message more approachable and memorable.

Their brand message might be something like, "Empowering people with autoimmune diseases to improve their health through whole-foods based nutrition."

In conclusion, having a consistent brand voice and message is important for establishing yourself as the go-to expert in your field.

By developing a voice and message that reflects who you are and what you stand for, you'll be able to connect with your target audience and build a strong brand that people will remember and trust.

Crafting a Compelling Book That Builds Your Brand

From Ideas to Pages

Now that you've got your niche, unique selling point (as we say in the Black culture "put your spit on it"), and brand voice and message figured out, it's time to start writing your book. ✍

Your book should be much more than just a collection of pages filled with information. It's an opportunity to establish yourself as the authority in your industry or niche, to connect with your target audience, and to build a strong brand that sets you apart from the competition. Keep this at the forefront of your mind as we sketch out your book.

Oh, did you think you were going to walk away from this book without one of your OWN??

Think of your book as the centerpiece of your personal branding strategy. It showcases your expertise, shares your unique perspective, and demonstrates your ability to provide value to your audience. And when you get your book in the hands of the right people, it can lead to new clients, more speaking engagements, and a steady stream of income.

Moreover, your book serves as a powerful marketing tool that can help you reach a wider audience and grow your business. With your book, you have the opportunity to promote your services, share your message, and connect with your target audience in a way that is both meaningful and memorable.

And best of all, your book never goes on vacation or takes a sick day! It's there 24/7, working tirelessly to promote your brand and build your business.

So if you're looking to establish yourself as an authority in your field, a book is the perfect tool to help you do just that.

📖

Developing Your Book Idea and Outlining Your Content

Before you put pen to paper (or fingers to keyboard), it's important to have a clear idea of what you want to cover in your book. This will help you stay focused and ensure that your book covers all the important information your audience needs to know.

To start, try brainstorming your main topics and organizing your ideas into an outline. This outline will serve as the blueprint for your book, helping you to stay focused and on track as you write. And if you ever get stuck, simply refer back to your outline to get back on track.

When developing your book idea and outlining your content, it's important to keep your target audience in mind. What are their needs? What problems are they facing? What questions do they have? By answering these questions, you'll be able to create a book that is both relevant and valuable to your audience.

Cha-ching money bags with purpose :)

Also, consider the *format* of your book. Will it be a how-to guide, a memoir, a collection of timeless recipes, or something else entirely? The format of your book can impact its content, so it's important to choose the right format for your message and audience.

Side Bar: Layout design is one of Black Seeds Publishing's specialties!! Our book layout designs are unique, beautiful and jaw dropping!

Check out our latest designs on our website, which is also beautifully designed and managed by Black Seeds Publishing. Contact us if YOU want to stand out in your industry, too! Let us design for you...

To make the process of developing your book idea and outlining your content even easier, try using a template or outline template. These templates provide a structure for your book, and can help you organize your thoughts and ideas in a logical and straightforward way.

And, of course, on my website, I put MY very own book template on there for self-publishing authors to get it right the first time :)

If you don't want to figure it out the long-do it yourself, watch a buttload of tube videos-way, use my template!

And because you purchased this book, you can have it for FREE, with this **coupon code**:

WRITENOW77

www.blackseedspublishing.com

So, get those creative juices flowing and start brainstorming your book idea today! 💡

With a clear idea of what you want to cover and a solid outline in place, you'll be well on your way to crafting a compelling book that builds your brand. 💪

📖

For our nutritionist, their book idea may be to write a guide on using whole foods to improve gut health and support the immune system for people with autoimmune diseases.

They would then create an outline that covers the main topics, such as the importance of gut health, how certain foods can support or harm the gut, and the steps to take to improve gut health through food.

Writing Your Book

The juice.

The reason you are here.

Now it's time to start writing, or what I like to call, "throwing up on paper!"

Success Tip #2

"Hire an expert. Writing ain't for everybody and most visionaries suck at writing copy that will sell their product or service. So hire an expert in that field that can convey your heart into dollars. There are budget-friendly independent content creators that specifically serves small businesses on a budget. That's how I got my start."

- Jamie Hopkins

Remember to use your brand voice and message, and make sure your writing is engaging and informative. Use anecdotes and examples to illustrate your points and make your content more memorable.

You've got your book idea, you've outlined your content, now it's time to start writing! And while writing a book can seem like a daunting task, it's important to remember that you don't have to write the whole thing in one sitting.

Take your time and break the process down into manageable chunks. Write a little each day, or set aside time each week to work on your book. And if you get stuck, don't be afraid to take a break and come back to it later.

When it comes to writing your book, there are a few things to keep in mind:

Write in your brand voice: Your book is a reflection of your brand, so make sure that your writing style and tone are consistent with your brand's messaging and personality.

Make it engaging: Your book should be informative and educational, but it should also be entertaining. Use humor, storytelling, and other engaging techniques to keep your reader's attention and make your book a pleasure to read.

And please, for the sake of all humanity, no more snooze books! You know, the ones that make you go to sleep.

As a publisher, I'm fed up of overly technical-written books that loses the audience while only expressing the emotions and passion of the author/business owner. Perhaps you understand words that are 13 letters long, but your target audience need a lighter version. Make it engaging for THEM.

Provide value: Remember, your book should serve a purpose, so make sure that you're providing value to your reader. Share your expertise, offer tips and advice, and include helpful information that your reader can use.

Stay focused: It can be tempting to wander off-topic, but it's important to stay focused and keep your book on-topic. Keep your outline handy to help you stay on track and ensure that your book covers all the important information your audience needs to know.

Hire an expert: If all else fells, and all of this sounds like gibberish to you, hire a ghostwriter if your pocketbook or wallet affords. The really goods ones are pricey, but well worth it in terms of how you can get your "return on investment". Stay turned for more on that, too!

By following these tips, you'll be well on your way to writing a book that is both informative and enjoyable to read. And once you've finished writing, it's time to get your book out into the world so that *it* can start working for *you*!

Revising and Editing Your Book

Once you've finished writing, it's time to revise and edit your book. This is where you'll refine your writing, fix any errors, and make sure your content is clear and concise. You may want to consider hiring a professional editor to help you with this step. And I know one if you're looking... **wink, wink 😉

Fast forward to the near future and ...

Congratulations, you've written your book!

But now, it's time to take a step back and look at your book with a critical eye. This is the time to revise and edit your book, making sure that it's the best it can be before you send it out into the world.

Here are a few tips for revising and editing your book:

Take a break: Before you start revising and editing, it's important to take a break from your book. Give yourself some time to clear your head and come back to your book with fresh eyes.

Read it out loud: Reading your book out loud is a great way to catch any awkward phrasing, typos, or other mistakes. Plus, it helps you get a sense of the flow and pacing of your book.

Get feedback: Don't be afraid to ask for feedback from others. Share your book with friends, family, or even a distant colleague and get their thoughts and suggestions for improvement.

My take-it-or-leave-it-tip: Don't ask a professional editor or publisher for FREE advice. Even if you do have a personal relationship with them. If you can't afford for a consultation, then offer a bargaining chip. A $5 gift card for coffee or a bottle of her favorite wine... oh, sorry, I got sidetracked... my point is:

Don't go empty handed with your hands always out. There's a universal law on reaping what you sow, some cultures call it *karma*. ***-End of tip.-***

Focus on the details: Editing is all about the details. Look for typos, grammar mistakes, and other small errors that can detract from your book's overall quality.

Keep your brand in mind: As you revise and edit your book, make sure that you're staying true to your brand's voice and message. Your book should be a reflection of your brand, so make sure that it's consistent with your brand's personality and tone.

By following these tips, you'll be able to revise and edit your book to make it the best it can be. And once you're confident that your book is the best it can be, it's time to get it published and start building your brand!

Entrepreneurial Hard Knock Lesson #2

"There is no such thing as the perfect time to do something. Stop waiting until your kids are grown and out of the house, or your significant other shows interest and support, or whatever excuse you have settled on for not starting now. Let go of your excuses and launch the damn business already! You have so many tools available that it can cost you nothing... except your legacy."

- Jamie Hopkins

Making a Splash with Your Book and Building Your Following

Launch Day

It's finally here - launch day for your book! You've put in so much hard work to get to this point, and now it's time to make a splash and start building your following, or as I like to call them – your "tribe".

Your tribe is different from your target audience. Your target audience is who you're talking to, but your tribe are the ones who listened and took action! Let's build your tribe.

∞

Here are a few tips for making the most of your book launch:

Celebrate: Take a moment to celebrate this amazing accomplishment! You've written a book, and that's no small feat. It's equally important to acknowledge and appreciate all of the hard work that went into it. So, take a moment to enjoy the moment and pat yourself on the back.

"When I'm working with my clients at Black Seeds Publishing, "celebrate yourself" milestones are embedded inside or publishing process. I often encourage my clients along the way to celebrate every milestone, hence I call it "celebrate yourself". You get a better book that way."

-Jamie Hopkins

Have a party: Invite friends, family, and supporters to celebrate your launch. Whether it's a small gathering or a big bash, make sure to celebrate this special occasion with the people who matter most.

Treat yourself: Whether it's a spa day, a shopping spree, or a fancy dinner, treat yourself to something special to mark the occasion.

Reflect on your journey: Take a moment to reflect on the journey that led you to this point. *Write down* your thoughts and feelings, and appreciate all of the hard work and determination that went into writing your book.

💡 Tip: Review your written thoughts and feelings. Create writing prompts from your reflections. This journal that you just wrote (see how I did that?), send it to your publisher and create an accompanying journal or devotional to go along with your new book! Bam.. 2 products out of 1 (so far... keep reading, it gets better).

Share your success: Share your success with others, whether it's through social media, a blog post, or just a simple phone call. Letting others know about your accomplishment can be a great way to spread the word and *build momentum* for your launch.

🕐 **Timeline: 2 weeks**

By celebrating your book launch, you'll be able to acknowledge and appreciate your hard work, and *set the tone* for a successful launch and beyond. So, go ahead and celebrate! You've earned it!

Get the word out: Spread the word about your book launch. Reach out to your network and let everyone know that your book is now available (or pre-order).

Utilize your network: Reach out to your friends, family, and professional contacts to let them know about your book. Ask for their support in spreading the word and encourage them to share your book with their network as well.

Leverage social media: Social media is a powerful tool for getting the word out about your book launch. Share updates and teasers about your book, and make sure to use relevant hashtags to reach a wider audience.

Utilize email: Email is a great way to reach a large number of people quickly. Send an email blast to your subscribers, and make sure to include a link to your book's landing page.

I interrupt this program to make a bold statement: though we live in a world that is ever changing and technology is constantly revolving, do NOT discount the old school methods that have stood the test of time... **and that email list is where it's at.

Case in point, there are still people in today's time of this book being published, that has had the same telephone number since they owned a phone! They only had one phone number that never EVER changed. Meanwhile, I've had about 10 in my lifetime... and counting. And they, who should remain nameless, stand in the age bracket of mid-50s. That's a long commitment :)

Okay, second point to that point, there are people who still use their AOL email address for business purposes. In 2023 when the world has moved on to gmail and other major tech moguls.

What's my point? Use what works **and has worked** for more than 20 minutes, you dig?

Host a launch event: Consider hosting a launch event to celebrate your book launch. This could be a book signing, a talk, or even a virtual event. This will give your audience a chance to engage with you and learn more about your book. Thus building your tribe from your own vibe.

Partner with influencers: Partnering with influencers in your industry or niche can help you reach a wider audience. Consider reaching out to bloggers, YouTubers, or other influencers to see if they would be interested in sharing your book with their followers.

By utilizing a variety of strategies to get the word out about your book launch, you'll be able to reach a wider audience and build momentum for your launch. So, don't be shy! Share your book with the world!

Engage With Your Audience

Engaging with your audience is a crucial step in building your brand and establishing a strong following (or tribe). Here are some tips:

Respond to feedback: Respond to comments and feedback from your readers. Whether it's on social media, email, or in person, make sure to listen to what your audience has to say and respond in a thoughtful and engaging way.

Host Q&A sessions: Consider hosting Q&A sessions on social media or through a virtual platform to engage with your audience and answer their questions. This will give them an opportunity to learn more about you and your book, and provide you with valuable feedback.

Share additional content: Share additional content related to your book, such as blog posts, videos, or podcasts. This will give your audience a chance to dive deeper into your brand and learn more about your expertise.

Offer exclusive content: Offer exclusive content to your audience as a way of thanking them for their support. This could be a special report, a bonus chapter, or a live webinar.

Build a community: Consider building a community around your brand by creating a Facebook group, hosting events, or starting a newsletter. This will give your audience a place to connect and engage with one another, and with you.

Engage with your audience to establish your brand, create a community around your book, and cultivate a strong following. Don't keep your audience waiting - start engaging with them now!

Offer Incentives

Consider offering incentives for people who purchase your book during launch week. This could be something as simple as a discount or a free bonus, like a download of additional content.

Offering incentives to your audience is a great way to encourage them to engage with your brand and spread the word about your book. Here are some tips:

Giveaways: Host giveaways for copies of your book, merchandise, or other products related to your brand. This will create excitement and generate buzz around your book.

Early access: Offer early access to your book or exclusive content to your audience as a thank you for their support. This will give them a special behind-the-scenes look at your book and help build anticipation.

Discounts: Offer discounts on your book or merchandise to your audience. This is a great way to incentivize them to make a purchase and spread the word about your book.

Contests: Consider hosting contests related to your book, such as a writing contest or a photography contest. This will encourage your audience to get creative and engage with your brand in a fun way.

Loyalty rewards: Offer loyalty rewards to your audience for their support, such as a special bonus chapter, a live webinar, or a one-on-one call with you.

Offering incentives is a great way to encourage your audience to engage with your brand and spread the word about your book. So, get creative and start incentivizing!

Follow Up

After your launch, make sure to follow up with your audience. [THIS IS THE MOST OVERLOOKED INCOME STREAM!!! That follow up money bag].

Thank them for their support and ask for feedback. This will help you build a strong and engaged following. Here are some tips for following up:

Send a thank you note: Send a thank you note to your audience for their support. This can be a handwritten note, an email, or a message on social media. This small gesture will go a long way in building a strong relationship with your audience.

Keep them updated: Keep your audience updated on any news or updates related to your book, such as book signings, new releases, or events. This will keep them engaged and informed about your brand.

Ask for a review: Ask your audience to leave a review of your book on Amazon, Goodreads, or another platform. This will help build credibility and generate buzz around your book.

Engage on social media: Engage with your audience on social media by responding to comments, liking and sharing their posts, and participating in conversations. This will keep your audience engaged and help you build a strong online presence.

Offer more value: Offer your audience more value by providing them with additional resources, such as a free report, a bonus chapter, or a live webinar. This will help establish your brand as a leader in your industry and keep your audience engaged.

By following these tips, you'll be able to make a splash with your book launch and start building your following.

And with a strong following, you'll be well on your way to using your book to build a profitable business!

Using it to Grow Your Business and Reach More People

Maximizing Your Book's Potential

Now that your book is published and making a splash, it's time to take things to the next level. In this chapter, we'll explore ways to maximize the potential of your book and use it to grow your business and reach more people.

The Magic Formula: More Reach = More Impact

"A gift opens the way and ushers the giver into the presence of the great." -Proverbs 18:16 (Holy Bible, New International Version)

As an extreme introvert, I will be the FIRST to admit that it is uncomfortable talking about your own work sometimes. You have to promote yourSelf, and sometimes that's not easy to do.

You may come off too, overly confident or extremely shy and withdrawn. There's a perfect balance between what's public and what's kept private.

This is where you allow intuition to rule.

Repurposing Your Content

One of the best ways to maximize the potential of your book is to repurpose your content. You can use your book as the foundation for a variety of other content, such as blog posts, podcasts, webinars, and more. And I'm going to go a little deep into each in this section.

Bottom line: repurposing your content is a great way to maximize the potential of your book and reach a wider audience and here's how you can do it:

A. Blog Posts 📝

Take the key themes and ideas from your book and turn them into blog posts. You can also use your blog posts to promote your book and build buzz around it.

To take your blog to another level, monetize it! This is where affiliate networks are best utilized for authors. You can partner with book-related or even industry-related organizations or small businesses to further spread your reach and message.

Start making your topic list now! Here, if I was to do it, well... okay, here's a "sneak peak, behind-the-scenes" view of my very own Blog Post spreadsheet.

Tip: I keep a running blog/podcast topic list on a shared workspace to easily send off to my social media team. It keeps us all on the same page with promotions and other marketing campaigns.

There are platforms such as Notion, Trello, Asana, Monday and others that are great for small business project management (even if you are a solopreneur).

These tools help a business owner keep track of their business! Okay, enough babbling. Here's my own planning, slash, brainstorming, slash, data dump of everything on my heart Blog and Podcast Planning Template :) - say that 10 times fast.

Get a separate journal for your brainstorming ideas. Trust me, once you give yourself permission to imagine the unimaginable, ideas will flow quickly and you want to be sure you are ready to receive them.

Part 1: Overall Podcast/Blog Topic Schedule

Release Date	Record NLT Date	Guest	Topic	Offer
16 Dec	04 Dec	Host Only	The Case of Mistaken Identity	Store Discount: 10% Coupon: EVE20
23 Dec	11 Dec	K.M.	What Faith Looks Like in a Faithless World	Stepping Out On Faith Book
06 Jan	18 Dec	Sponsor	Why I Moved to Africa	Travel Journal

B. Podcasts 🎙

Turn your book into a podcast series. This will allow you to reach an audience who prefer to consume content in audio format, and give you an opportunity to discuss your book in greater detail.

I actually use my podcast to steer the wheel in conversation, then repurpose that content into a blog. I know this sounds like a lot, but honestly, I create one piece of content and repurpose that into many. It's math and science combined :)

Success Tip #3

"There are a million ways to make money from your book. Seriously. All it takes is for you to find what works for YOU and your lifestyle... then create as many of those babies (i.e. streams of income) as you want!"

- Black Seeds Publishing

Here's my very own podcast segment planning chart. As a storyteller, I blab a LOT, so this segment planner keeps me on time target and on topic.

Part 2: Podcast Segment Planning

Segment / Time	Topic	Notes	Length in Minutes
Opening Jingle / Intro / Segue		Pre-recorded	
Topic 1			15
Vocal Segue	Moving to next topic		
Topic 2			15
Ad Insertion		Pre-recorded**	
Segue #2	Moving to next topic		
Topic 3			15
Outro / Closing Jingle			

C. Webinars 🖥️

Host webinars to promote your book and reach a wider audience. Offer your audience a behind-the-scenes look at your book and the ideas it presents.

This will help you engage with your audience and build a strong connection with them.

D. Workshops 🎯

Host workshops to promote your book and reach a wider audience. Offer your audience the opportunity to dive deeper into the ideas presented in your book and engage with you in real-time.

For the storytellers, introverts who think this is out of your league, you have to "think" about it differently. Maybe it's not YOU directly teaching the workshops, but you've partnered with other business partners of like mind and spirit, who love to be on camera and in the spotlight, and they conduct the discussions around your book.

Whatever and however you choose to offer this product, it has proven to be a lucrative offer. Think about it, people are ALWAYS seeking knowledge.

There's a conscious society that wants to gain as much as knowledge as possible. Use your book as an educational tool to feed that industry of knowledge seekers.

Webinars will help you build a strong connection with your audience and establish your brand as a thought leader in your industry. Point blank.

By repurposing your content, you'll be able to reach a wider audience and establish your brand as a thought leader in your industry. So, get creative and make the most of your book!

Building Your Email List

Got a list?

I'm back again with this "old school" method. But time has proven that building an email list is a key component of growing your business and reaching more people. Offer your audience an incentive, such as a free report or a bonus chapter, in exchange for their email address.

This will help you build a list of engaged and interested followers who are eager to hear from you.

I know it sounds like I'm being repetitive here. And I am intentionally. It's a part of how you learn... through repetition and action.

FULL DISCLOSURE: I never really took advantage of this "passive income stream" in the start of my entrepreneurial journey. I just didn't know what to "say" in those emails, and I was such a touchy feely person, that I was stuck for years on this one income.

I have countless email sequence copy written and saved on my computer. Never used not a one! To be honest, I felt like the email marketing, any marketing for that matter, "tricked" people into making a purchase... and I wanted to genuinely draw people to me. So I refused to sound robotic or "like everybody else"...

It was all an illusion. MY illusion that I made up for myself and believed it. I created this fear and it became real to me.

I lost millions because of my fear.

Millions.

I'll leave it at that.

Enough of that... here's how you can build that money list:

A. Offer a Free Resource 

Offer your audience a free resource, such as a chapter from your book or a related guide, in exchange for their email address. This will help you grow your email list and build a relationship with your audience.

Readers love to read, so the more you feed them for free, they will eat. Be careful how MUCH you share for free. Instead of an entire chapter, pull out powerful sections and share that for free. Trust yourself to know this boundary. You will instinctually know when "enough is enough".

B. Host a Contest

Host a contest and offer a prize for those who sign up for your email list. The prize does not have to cost you a dime to give away, or bares a minimum cost such as a cup of coffee. I would suggest the prize resembles a connection to the message of the book :)

C. Leverage Your Social Media Following 

How many times do I have to say this? The #1 FREE tool available to anyone, anywhere at anytime.

Leverage your social media following to grow your email list. Encourage your followers to sign up for your email list by offering them *exclusive content*, such as a sneak peek at your upcoming book or a chance to star in your next fiction book.

Okay, so by now, I've mentioned social media 13 times :) It's technology and it's ever changing but the largest and well-known platforms may be here to stay for a while - at least until this book is published! So let's take a closer look at some of the current social media platforms and how they are being used:

PLATFORM	DESCRIPTION	DEMOGRAPHIC
Goodreads www.goodreads.com	A social platform for book lovers where authors can connect with readers, share must-read books, and host discussions. Goodreads has an awesome giveaway program for book launches too. Check them!	Used by a diverse demographic of avid readers and book enthusiasts from various age groups.

Facebook	A popular social networking site where authors can start a group/ community, host book launches, do livestream with other authors or	Has a diverse user base, but it is most popular among adults aged 25 to 54.
Twitter	A microblogging platform that allows authors to share short updates and engage with readers.	Attracts a broad demographic, but it is particularly popular among millennials and professionals.
Instagram	A visual-centric platform where authors can share images and videos related to their book.	Predominantly used by younger audiences, particularly those aged 18 to 34.
YouTube / TikTok / Instagram Reels / Facebook Stories	A video-sharing platform where authors can create video content, book trailers, and author interviews.	Has a diverse user base, but it is widely used by younger generations and those seeking video-based content.
Pinterest	A visual discovery platform that allows authors to share book covers, inspirations, and recommendations.	Has a predominantly female user base, with a significant number of users aged 18 to 49.
LinkedIn	A professional networking platform where authors can connect with industry professionals and promote their book.	Primarily used by professionals, business owners, and those seeking career-related content.

💡 Visit some of your favorite authors social media platforms and see what is current. Check out those competitors too... trust me, you may see a trend of how most book funnels are set up. Yes, I said the "f" word. We'll circle back to that later.

D. Offer a Subscriber-Only Newsletter 

Offer a subscriber-only newsletter to those on your email list. Building an email list is essential to maximizing the potential of your book and growing your business.

So, make sure to put these strategies into action and watch your email list go up up up!

Hosting Workshops and Webinars

Hosting workshops and webinars is another great way to maximize the potential of your book and reach more people. Offer your audience the opportunity to learn more about your book and the ideas it presents, and engage with them in real-time.

This recommendation is for those who are excellent educators! Another niche that goes undercover and underrated.

Education is the backbone of our existence. It's how we teach each other to survive and keep the Earth moving. So why not be a part of that evolution and "teach one, each one".

Don't try to do every single recommendation! Pick out the ones that feel comfortable to you and your following.

Not everyone is a webinar presenter, perhaps you're an introvert like me and would rather gain a following through a referral network. I have such a strong referral network, but that's a story for another day.

Creating a Product Line

You need something to sell other than your book and accompanying journal. By creating complementary products, you can offer your audience a complete solution to their problem and provide them with additional value. Here are some examples of products you can create:

A. Courses and E-Learning 🖥️

Create a course or an e-learning platform that teaches your audience the same content as your book in a more structured and comprehensive way. You can offer this as an upgrade to your book or as a standalone product.

B. Coaching and Consulting 📲

Offer one-on-one coaching or consulting services to your audience. This will give them the opportunity to receive personalized guidance from you and help them achieve their goals more quickly.

C. Physical Products 📚

Create physical products that complement your book, such as workbooks, journals, or planners. These products will give your audience a way to apply the information from your book and help them retain the information.

By creating a product line (i.e. income stream), you can provide your audience with additional value and grow your business.

So, think about what products you can create that will complement your book and take your business to the next level!

Here's a list of common products and services offered by authors. This is NOT a comprehensive list, but something to get your creative juices flowing.

Low Cost Value	Medium Cost Value	High Cost Value
E-books	Online Courses	Personal Coaching
Audiobooks	Workbooks	VIP Memberships
Print-on-Demand Merchandise	Webinars	Exclusive Events
Digital Downloads	Consulting Services	Retreats
Merchandise (e.g., T-shirts, mugs)	Mastermind Groups	Author Mentoring
Online Community Memberships	Premium Content Subscriptions	Speaking Engagements
Short Stories or Novellas	Group Coaching	Personalized Retreats
Companion Guides	Self-Publishing Services	Writing Workshops
Exclusive Interviews	Writing Retreats	Publishing Packages
Reader Discussion Guides	Content Editing Services	Literary Agent Representation

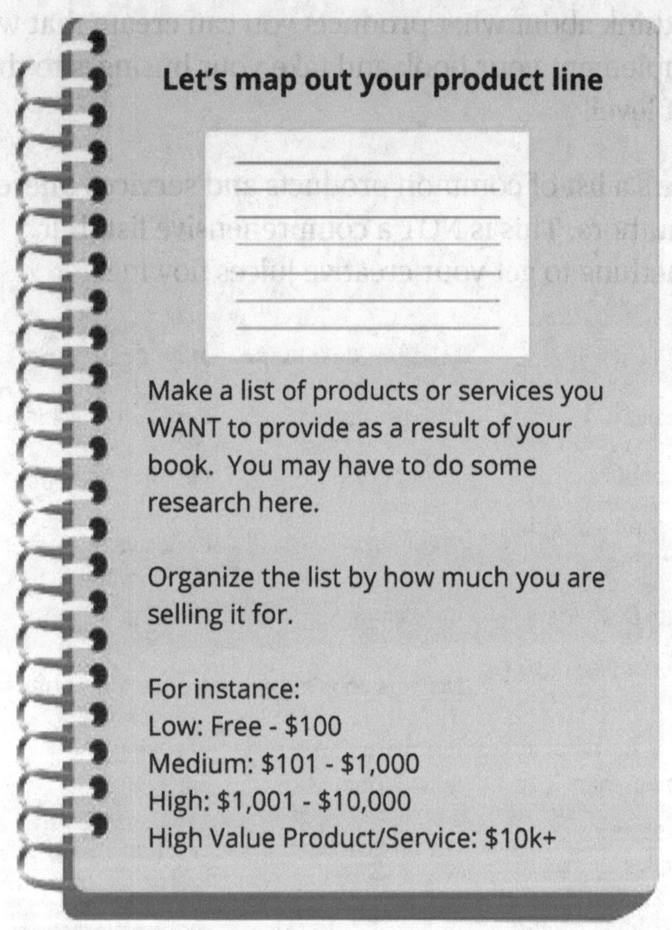

Now, sit this product list to the side. You'll need it later when it's time to develop your profit plan. It's this list that you're going to offer to your tribe. The solutions to their problems in a way that you can deliver it rightly.

Simple as that.

Now, brace yourself. The next headline will seem ... a bit repetitive. But it needs to be said.

 Extra Extra Read all About It: LEADS 

Leads, Leads, Leads!

The worm that hooks the fish.

The grease that keeps the wheel turning.

You can't have a business if you don't have leads.

Ok, so let's start with what the heck is a "lead". A lead, in simplest terms, is someone who is interested in your product, service, movement, mission, purpose. They indicate their interest by responding to whatever you present before them - whether it is a post on Facebook or a click on your website.

Leads come in all different shapes and sizes. And a good lead takes the form of the product or service for which it attracts the interest. In other words, create a lead magnet to draw the type of customer you want to serve.

Hence, a book can be the lead magnet to your business story and your audience. It is the connector, the book that is. It connects your brand to your audience.

Here's my very own lead magnet that I use for the publishing side of the house:

Download your free copy at bit.ly/writenow77
(Take note of the "call to actions" inside my lead magnet)

Taking Your Brand to the Next Level with Your Book

The Future Is Bright

Congratulations! You've written a book that has established your authority and credibility in your industry, and you've taken advantage of its potential to grow your business. But your journey doesn't have to end here.

In this chapter, we'll talk about how you can continue to leverage your book to take your brand to the next level.

Keep Writing

Writing more books is a great way to continue to establish your authority and reach a wider audience. You can write books on similar topics or branch out into new areas. Just keep writing and your audience will continue to grow.

💡 Tip: Refer back to your topic list you made earlier during the writing process. You have more books inside of you than you realize. Just make a plan, stick to it and watch it grow. Period.

Stay Connected

Stay connected with your audience by maintaining an active presence on social media and other platforms. Respond to their comments and questions, and continue to engage with them. This will help you build a loyal following and keep your brand top of mind.

💡 Tip: Okay, for you introverts like myself, this is the hardest part of the job: talking to folks. Well, I built an entire no-contact business (after being burnt so many times by my own people) that runs like a smooth baby bottom! There are other online platforms that are more protective than the ones that are filled with the unpleasant kind, so do your research and find the right match for you and your lifestyle. You may have to kiss a few frogs along the way.

Collaborate

Collaborating with other authors, influencers, and experts in your industry will give you the opportunity to reach new audiences and learn new things. Seek out partnerships and collaborations that will help you grow your brand and reach more people.

It's also the quickest way to grow your own audience by borrowing the influence of the one who went before you. Guess what, YOU are the same influence for someone else... so keep that in mind as you form relationships in this business.

Experiment

Don't be afraid to experiment and try new things. Whether it's a new marketing strategy or a new product line, always be open to exploring new opportunities. This will help you stay ahead of the curve and continue to grow your brand.

The future is bright, and the opportunities for growth are endless. Keep using your book as a foundation for your brand, and you'll be well on your way to taking it to the next level.

So, go out there and make the most of your book, movement, message!

Once I told my story–as ugly and unattractive as it was–I freed myself from the trauma and guilt of the past, thus allowing me to enjoy life again.

- Jamie Hopkins

The Art of Using Your Book to Tell Your Story and Build Your Legacy

Chapter And Verse

Your book is more than just a tool for building your brand, it's a way to tell your story and build your legacy. In this chapter, we'll explore the art of using your book to do just that.

Storytelling

Your book is an opportunity to share your story, your journey, and your wisdom with the world. A well-told story can be powerful and inspiring, and it can help you connect with your audience on a deeper, more impactful, level... life-changing even. I mean, your story changed YOUR life :)

I digress...

Here, case in point: One successful entrepreneur used her book to tell the story of how she built her business from the ground up. She shared the ups and downs of her journey, and the lessons she learned along the way. This not only inspired her readers, but it also helped her establish her brand as a thought leader in her industry.

This could be YOU. For some of you reading this book, it IS you. You've already learned to master this art of using your story to build your brand.

💡 Tip: You're a writer now... you don't have to tell YOUR story. Use your gifts to write other people's stories (with their permission of course). One word: Ghostwriter.

Legacy Building

Your book is a way to leave a lasting legacy, something that will continue to inspire and educate people long after you're gone. Use your book to share your values, your vision, and your mission with the world.

Another case in point: A business leader wrote a book about his leadership philosophy, and how he built his company with a focus on integrity, transparency, and service to others. This book not only served as a testament to his values, but it also inspired other business leaders to adopt a similar philosophy. Today, his company is known for its strong culture, and his book is still considered a must-read for anyone looking to build a successful and ethical business.

The Bible is known as one of the oldest books in history, but let me tell you that it is not the ONLY. There are ancient texts we are still reading and gaining knowledge and inspiration from in modern today.

Legacy is about leaving that fabric of existence and continuing the story of our DNA... our bloodline. This book is part of my own legacy. Over the years, I've gained so much intellectually, spiritually, physically, financially, emotionally, and even metaphysically. All of that is weaved throughout the pages of this book.

Inspiration

Your book can inspire others to take action and make a difference in their own lives and in the world. Share your passion, your vision, and your message with the world and you'll leave a lasting impact.

You guessed it, another case in point (I got tons of them): A motivational speaker wrote a book about how to find your purpose and live a fulfilling life. This book inspired countless people to pursue their passions and live the life they always dreamed of. The author continues to tour the world, speaking to packed audiences and spreading his message of hope and inspiration.

Chapter and verse, your book is a tool for telling your story, building your legacy, and inspiring others. So don't hold back, use it to make a difference in the world.

You would be surprised at what people write books about these days. I always lead with integrity and purpose. Everything else flows naturally and continually...

Strategies for Continual Growth and Success with Your Book

Writing the Next Chapter

So, you've written a successful book that has established your authority and credibility, and helped you grow your business. But the journey doesn't end here. In fact, it's just the beginning. To ensure continued success and growth, it's important to have a strategy in place for the future. In this chapter, we'll explore some *strategies* for keeping your brand and your business growing and thriving!

👉 Stay on Top of Your Niche

Keep up-to-date with the latest developments in your industry or niche. Read books, attend conferences, and network with other experts to stay informed and continue to grow your knowledge.

"Always be learning," I can't remember where I've heard it before or even who said it but it is worth repeating here. Never stop learning. Why? Because the world is constantly evolving and if you're not keeping up with the trends, you'll get left behind. Case in point: Blockbuster. When Netflix hit the scene and people didn't have to leave their homes anymore to return late videos.... It was a fast and quick R.I.P. buster.

👉 Keep Your Brand Fresh

Regularly update your book and your brand messaging to keep them current and relevant. Don't be afraid to change things up and try new things, but always keep your unique selling proposition and brand voice consistent.

And for goodness sake, you can launch your book more than once! I have past clients that launched their book (which was an amazingly powerful book) one time, and put it one the shelf ever since. There's a message that has gone as far as my publishing and editing staff. It's a sad experience that I see often and hopefully, this book will ignite that fire and get those messages back where they belong: off the shelf in into the world! [You should know that I am resisting the urge to insert the "eyeball emoji" right here...]

👉 Diversify Your Offerings

Consider expanding your product line to include additional books, courses, webinars, or coaching services. The more you have to offer, the more opportunities you have to reach new audiences and grow your business.

Yes, I've said this before in earlier chapters. I'll probably say it again later. At this point, from the earlier verse, you should already have your list ready. If you don't, here's a second chance to get that list!

Your book can lead to so many other products: more books, and each book having it's own stream of revenue, including merchandise. One of my favorite products that can carry a strong message of your movement or book is your very own magazine! I didn't take advantage of this stream of revenue just yet, but I was definitely sponsored in several!

I hope you're picking up what I'm dropping: the world is your oyster. Your imagination is your only limitation.

👉 Engage With Your Audience

Continuously engage with your readers and followers, responding to their questions and comments and seeking their feedback. This will help you build a loyal following and keep your brand top-of-mind.

A common way of keeping this engagement is hosting book readings at your local library (community involvement is key to building a local fanbase). Another common engagement tool (and my absolute favorite) is podcast.

I'm an extreme introvert (did I say that already?), and so podcasting was a no-brainer for me! I could monetize my message and not show my face at the same time. Winning!

And if you don't want to run your own podcast, be a guest on others... just make sure you do your homework and check out that podcaster's brand message and reputation.

At the time of this book being published, there was one popular website where you can search different podcasts based on topic to become a guest on their show: www.podcastguests.com.

👉 Collaborate With Others

Partner with other experts in your industry or niche to reach new audiences and offer new and exciting products and services. Consider other related industries that you can collaborate with as well.

For example, an author can collaborate with local bookstores, libraries, and coffee shops to host events. You're bringing in business to their establishments so many of them are eager for such partnerships and collaborations.

This can help you expand your reach and grow your business in new and exciting ways.

👉 Give Back

Use your book and your business to give back to your community. This could be through charitable donations, volunteering your time and expertise, or creating products and services that help people in need.

I started a program where all of the proceeds earned through the publishing side of the house goes back into a Black, Brown, Melanated, Indigenous owned business. It's called appropriately, Black Seeds and you can find out how to apply for free, at the time of this publication, at www.blackseedspublishing.com.

👉 Keep Writing

Finally, keep writing! Duh! Of course you knew I was going to say this. Write new books, blog posts, and other content to keep your brand fresh and relevant and to continue growing your audience.

Become a self-publishing author who writes for a living. Or better yet, become a publisher of other people's works! We need more good publishers in this field and you have an excellent model to follow! Hint. Hint. :)

Wait, did somebody say, "How do I become a self-publishing author?" Well, I got just the toolbox to set you up for extreme success in the Indie Author industry (psssst... that's the fancy term for a self-

Get a digital copy at
www.blackseedspublishing.com

published author, except *they* make writing a lifestyle - not a hobby or one-hit wonder).

By following these strategies and continuously growing and evolving, you can ensure that your book and your brand continue to be a source of success and growth for years to come.

Case Study: For example, let's take the author and entrepreneur Tim Ferriss. He started out as a successful author with his book "The 4-Hour Work Week," which established his authority in the productivity and lifestyle design space. Since then, he has continued to write and publish new books, such as "Tools of Titans" and "Tribe of Mentors," and has diversified his offerings to include a podcast, blog, and courses. He has also collaborated with other experts in his niche and given back by supporting various charitable causes. By following some of the strategies mentioned in this book, Tim has *continued* to grow his brand and his business, establishing himself as a leading voice in his industry.

The moral of this story: if it works, work it.

How Referrals Can Boost Your Business Profits

The Power of Word of Mouth

Have you ever heard the saying, "the best form of advertising is word of mouth"? Well, it's true! Word of mouth referrals are one of the most powerful marketing tools for any business, big or small.

In fact, studies have shown that people are four times more likely to buy from someone they've been referred to by a friend. So, if you're looking to grow your business and increase your profits, referrals should definitely be a part of your marketing strategy.

Entrepreneurial Hard Knock Lesson #3

"99.9% of my publishing business came through my referral network. I built a strong, powerful, private network based on one service: integrity. My word is bond. If I can't do it, I won't pursue it. And money has NEVER been my motivator... healing has always been at the forefront. So my message to you is: be you, don't compromise on your morals and don't apologize for your decisions. Period."

- Jamie Hopkins

Now, you may be thinking, "But how do I get people to refer me to their friends and family?" The answer is simple: by providing excellent service, delivering quality products, and creating a fantastic customer experience.

When you consistently go above and beyond for your customers' expectations, they will naturally want to share your business with others.

Another way to encourage referrals is by offering incentives. This could be as simple as offering a discount on their next purchase for every referral they bring in, or offering a prize for the person who refers the most people.

People LOVE getting a good deal, and when you make it easy and attractive for them to refer their friends to your business, they're more likely to do it.

Another way to get referrals is by asking for them. Don't be afraid to ask your happy customers if they know anyone who could benefit from your products or services. People are often more than happy to help, especially when they've had a positive experience with your business.

Funny Story

Laughter is good for the soul - said someone wise

So for years I struggled in my business with marketing. I struggled with my personality of being an introvert, my spiritual journey of being a healer, and this reality of bills bills bills. I needed money. But being a healer AND an introvert AND an entrepreneur didn't work too well in the business world, so I thought.

With marketing, you HAD to talk to people and CONVINCE them to buy your product or service.

Ergo my problem – *convincing* people to buy. I felt it was a manipulation of the mind, playing with and on other people's feelings, and it just felt dirty. The conflict was with my soul purpose trying to "fit in".

Thus I decided to go a different route: just tell the damn truth. I refused to lie to my clients. I refused to over-promise and under-deliver. I was super transparent with my business practices (a little TOO transparent which later bit me in the ass, but that's a story for....).

I served from my heart, with all of my heart, standing firm on my principles. Sometimes, I even turned people DOWN because it just didn't feel right to me. I allowed my Spirit to guide me in the clients I selected for my business.

And in doing so, I built strong referral network. My clients trust me and allows me to serve them from a place where I know how. It's such a network that, when my business began to grow and I hired staff to take over the design department, certain unnamed clients *refused* to allow anyone else to work on their projects!

Yes, they demanded that only I design their book covers or workbooks or planners or whatever... Maybe I spoiled them a little, but my point is... after being told over and over that you cannot be successful as an honest spiritual healer in this industry, my story is proof that - that is a bunch of malarky!

📖

In summary, referrals are a valuable tool for growing your business and boosting your profits.

By providing excellent service, offering incentives, and asking for referrals, you can tap into the power of word of mouth and see your business soar!

YOUR BOOK

FROM IDEA TO EMPIRE

IS YOUR

FAMILY GENERATIONAL WEALTH

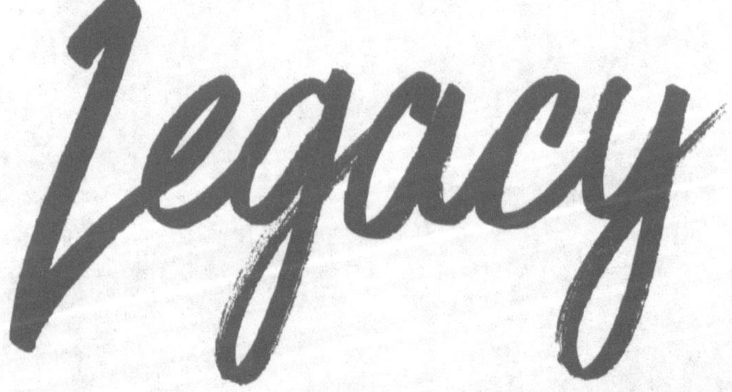

WRITTEN BY

JAMIE HOPKINS

CEO, BLACK SEEDS PUBLISHING & SERIAL ENTREPRENEUR

"An entrepreneur is someone who jumps off a cliff and builds a plane on the way down."

- Reid Hoffman

Tips for Maintaining Productivity and Reducing Stress

Client Management

So, you've done it! You've built a successful business with your book serving as the foundation of your brand. You've got clients coming in left and right and it's an amazing feeling! But as any business owner knows, managing clients can be a real challenge.

The last thing you want is for all of your hard work to be derailed by burnout or stress. That's why in this chapter, we're going to talk about some strategies for managing your clientele to keep stress levels low and productivity high.

📖

First, let's talk about the importance of having a **system in place**. Whether it's a physical system, like a binder or a digital system, like a project management tool, having a way to keep track of your clients and their needs is essential. It will help you stay organized and ensure that nothing falls through the cracks.

💡 Tip: One of the best project management tools at the time of this publication is Dubsado! I use it faithfully in my business because it has everything client management related built in one place. I can keep track of my clients, because it one has their own "portal".

Automated email, invoicing and payment options are just the tip of the iceberg of the many functions of this system, not to mention that it is super user-friendly. To learn more, go to my website where I stash all of my favorite business tools: www.blackseedspublishing.com.

Thank me later because I just saved hours in your day!

📖

Next, it's important to **set clear boundaries**. This can mean setting limits on the number of clients you take on, the hours you work, or the types of services you offer. It's important to be honest with yourself and your clients about what you can handle, and to stick to those boundaries.

💡 Keep in mind that your physical and spiritual health is just as important as your financial health. So take care of the WHOLE you, not just your business. Make time for self-care.

📖

Another key to successful client management is **good communication**. Make sure to set expectations from the start, and be clear about what you can and can't do for your clients.

Regular check-ins can also help keep things on track, and provide you with an opportunity to address any issues before they become bigger problems.

💡 Tip: Set up an email sequence with these check-ins so that both you and the client remain on track with the progress of your work. Automate, automate, automate! Every part of your business process (or customer journey) can be automated to save you time and stress!

📖

Finally, don't be afraid to **delegate**. Whether it's hiring an assistant or outsourcing certain tasks, delegating can help take some of the pressure off and give you more time to focus on what you do best.

Listen, we all know that managing clients can be a challenge, but with the right systems, clear boundaries, good communication, and delegation, you can keep stress levels low and productivity high.

By taking care of yourself, you'll be able to focus on growing your business and reaching even more people with your book.

"Where you find honey, you also find the bee."

\- Ghanian Proverb

The Importance of Building a Lasting Legacy for Future Generations

Leaving a Legacy

Have you ever thought about what you want to leave behind after you're gone?

Your book is not just a tool for building your brand and growing your business - it can also be a lasting legacy for future generations. That's why I wanted to spend a little more time about this word: Legacy.

📖

First, let's talk about why having a legacy is so important. A legacy is a way to pass down your values, beliefs, and experiences to future generations. It allows you to leave a lasting impact on the world and makes your life feel more meaningful.

And what better way to do that than through a book? A book is a *permanent record of your story* and can be passed down for generations to come.

But what makes a legacy truly special is its emotional impact. When you write a book that is not only informative, but also emotionally captivating, it can have a profound impact on those who read it.

Think about the books that have had a lasting impact on you - the ones that have inspired you, moved you to tears, or simply made you think. That's the kind of impact you can have with your book.

📖

Can I be honest? I mean, you have to promise you won't get mad, and continue reading...

Promise? Okay, the truth of the matter is...

You don't have to be *famous* to leave a legacy!

When I think legacy, I think about the single father who would buy old broken down cars, rebuild them with his hands and his own money, then give them away for free to families in need. He never received one penny or told anyone what he had done. And he often had to do it behind his pastor's back! **Legacy**.

When I think legacy, I think about the single mother of an active teenager who masters every sport he plays, so you know his extracurricular activities are not cheap. This single mother built an empire by investing in land in Africa where she is further building an industrial city for the local community. Her son is co-heir to the property. **Legacy**.

When I think legacy, I think about the wife and mother of three, who works tirelessly for someone else's dreams – I'm talking 32 hours a day – yet find the time to cook a full 8-course meal from scratch for her family at the end of a long day, and she does it with delight and joy! You see, she has the gift of sight so every business idea she launches... well, Mr. Kanye

West said it best: everything I throw up, blow up! **Legacy**.

When I think legacy, I think about the mother of an active 2-year-old, who also has endometriosis – a reproductive condition that causes women extreme pain during menstruation. An indescribable pain, and at the time of this publication, there is no cure.

But she pushes through her pain, chases a 2-year-old around while building her own business around reproductive healthcare for women with reproductive issues. By the time you read this, it will be her work that found a cure for women like me who deal with painful periods. Period. **Legacy**.

When I think legacy, I think about the wife, mother, sister, daughter and product of incest. She spent her entire childhood being passed from one pervert to another. Her uterus destroyed. Today, she healed from her trauma, became a mother of three, got a good husband that adores her and a family of unwavering faith. She rose from the ashes. She wrote her first book and it was the highest selling book to date that my company published! **Legacy**.

When I think legacy, I think about the husband and father of four. The only breadwinner in the family. Spends hours at his computer building a life changing legacy for his country. With one income, he put all of his kids through private school, raised them with honor and pride in their heritage, provided without fail to his family and country. You can't talk about Ghana without seeing work he's published online about this great land. Development projects are being birthed from this man's work. **Legacy**.

During my journey, I've met countless of people from different parts of the world who often felt like their story wasn't good enough for a book.

Can you believe that?

They felt that no one would read their book, no one would support them, no one would care.

Yet, those same individuals inspired me beyond words. They were my angels along the way. They were my guiding Light in most cases. Yet, they didn't see that about themselves. I saw Legacy, they saw death, pain or sorrow.

Now, you've come to the REAL reason why I wanted to write this book. The people I described above are not the only Legacies I've met along my nomadic journey.

But just with these few, combined with our skills, talents, gifts, can build our own city AND run it well!

You've heard of Black Wall Street haven't you? One day, I sat down and took inventory of my melanated friends and wrote down all of their skills, talents, gifts that I knew. This is what I found, among just a handful of my friends, are:

- Accountants/Finance
- Banking / Crypto Experts
- Educators/Historians
- Domestic Workers
- Painters
- Clerical/Administrative
- Agriculture/Agribusiness Experts
- Naturalists/Herbalists
- Agriculturalists / Farmers
- Scientists
- Reiki Practicians/Spiritual Healers
- Chefs/Cooks/Food Management
- Realtors/Land Owners
- Builders/Architects
- Carpenters/Plumbers
- Car Mechanics
- Engineers
- Electricians
- Movie Directors/Producers
- Film/Photographers
- Singers/Vocalists/Musicians
- Artists
- Video Editors
- Publishers
- Writers/Editors
- Graphic Designers
- Content Creators/ Visionaries
- Government Contractors
- Life/Business/Spiritual Coaches
- Ministers/Evangelists/ Prophets
- Digital Marketers
- Web Designers / App Developers
- Philanthropists

Legacy.

Legacy is not about being rich and famous, it's about the change and impact you are making today that will be our tomorrow.

So, let's get started on creating a legacy that will stand the test of time and inspire future generations.

With your book as your guide, you can leave a lasting impact on the world that will endure for years to come.

To learn more about Black Seeds and the marketplace we are building with and for Black-owned businesses, go to www.blackseedspublishing.com/seedprogram

Bank. Your. Book.

Bottom Line

A book works in ANY industry!

Congratulations! You've made it to the end of THIS book and what a journey it has been!

By now, you should have a solid understanding of how to use your book to build your brand and make a lasting impact in your industry.

From finding your niche, to crafting a compelling book, to launching it with a splash, to maximizing its potential, and finally to creating your legacy, you now have the tools you need to succeed.

But, before you close the pages of this book, let's recap what you've learned and offer some final tips to help you "bank your book."

📖

First, remember the power of your unique selling proposition (USP). Your USP sets you apart from the competition and makes your book, and therefore your brand, memorable to readers.

Next, don't be afraid to think outside the box when it comes to promoting your book. You've learned about the power of referrals, repurposing your content, building your email list, and even creating a product line, so put these strategies into action and see what works best for you.

When it comes to client management, always keep in mind the importance of balance. Make sure to prioritize your well-being and take breaks when necessary. This will not only help keep your stress levels down but also increase your productivity in the long run.

Your legacy is just as important as your book. Make sure you are creating something that not only helps you achieve your goals, but also has a positive impact on future generations. Your book is not just a means to an end, it is also a representation of who you are and what you stand for.

Bottom line: your book is your brand, and your brand is your legacy.

Use this book as a guide to help you reach your full potential and make an impact that will last for generations to come.

Good luck and remember, anything is possible if you put your mind to it!

About the Author

Under the umbrella of Black Seeds, LLC, I am a Freelance Content Creator on a mission to remove racial boundary lines within the indigenous people through education of our history, culture, belief and ecosystem through the use of literary arts.

I am an activist for re-writing history while printing what will last a lifetime. And I also want us as a people to show up in the marketplace in excellence!

SPECIALIZATIONS:

- Ghostwriting
- Content editing
- Book layout design
- Book cover design
- Digital product design
- Digital marketing
- Print and web design
- Video editing
- Global distribution network

Black Seeds Publishing is NOT on social media like most thriving businesses. We have two ways of communication: Word of Mouth and Website (www.blackseedspublishing.com).

Our mission is to create a safe economic environment for our black-owned, indigenous-owned, melanated skinned family. Every business is vetted through the proper legal channels, thus solidifying our value in the marketplace.

Spread the word. Sign your family up for Black Seeds and let's grow together, one seed at a time.

Get to know me: www.blackseedspublishing.com

Contact me: support@blackseedspublishing.com

Get started: bit.ly/applyblackseeds

Recommendations

If you want to laugh your butt off, follow my lifestyle blog at www.afrikanastories.com. It gets a little wild and crazy over there and it's for grown folks ONLY.

Subscribe to my podcast for women, The Eve Series, at https://podcasters.spotify.com/pod/show/afrikanastories48

For daily inspiration and tips, subscribe to my YouTube channel (literally if you want to raise your vibrations and be empowered every single day): https://youtube.com/@AfrikanaStories

My very first NFT collection was inspired by my own journey of healing and reinvention. Read Lola's story and see if there's anything in her story to inspires you in yours. View the collection:

https://opensea.io/collection/blackseeds-collection

My Other Books

Available in the shop at www.afrikanastories.com

Shop our merch, books, ebooks, journals, cookbooks and more! Each purchase supports another Black-owned business. Thank you!

My NFT Collection

My very first NFT Collection is now available! "Lola's Journey: A Celebration of Indigenous Resilience and Creativity" is a collection of four stunning NFTs that celebrate the resilience, strength, and creativity of indigenous women. Each piece of digital art captures a different moment in Lola's life - from her battle with vertigo and her struggles with abuse and addiction to her rediscovery of her roots and her bold and confident approach to life.

But Lola is more than just a collection of beautiful and unique NFTs. It's a tribute to the resilience and creativity of indigenous women everywhere. That's why a portion of the proceeds from every Lola NFT sale will go towards supporting another indigenous community in need. By adding Lola to your collection, you're not just getting a piece of digital art - you're joining a movement to celebrate and uplift indigenous voices and cultures and a community of people who are passionate about making a difference.

Don't miss your chance to own a piece of this inspiring collection. Join the movement today and experience the power of Lola for yourself.

For more information, visit www.blackseedspublishing.com/collection

Join Black Seeds

Black Seeds is an affiliate program consisting of Black-owned businesses and individuals whom I've met along my nomadic journey. And if all of these Black Seeds were gathered in one place, one garden, there's no limit to what we can build!

We are our own ecosystem, but rather than just talking about what we can build together, I am providing the platform (the marketplace) to do it! At NO COST TO THE SEEDS.

The SeedProgram is NOT an open forum where anyone can join. Instead, the SeedProgram is an invite-only platform, where only a previous Black Seed can invite another (vetted) Black or Brown-Skinned Owned Business. As a matter of fact, BSP will probably be the first business NOT on social media! You will only find us on online at our website, our own marketplace. Period. (I told you I'm an extreme introvert!)

In essence, Black Seeds mission statement is such: We are a social capital, socially conscious, spiritually adept premier Indigenous marketplace.

That's us. That's Black Seeds.

For more information, visit
www.blackseedspublishing.com/seedprogram

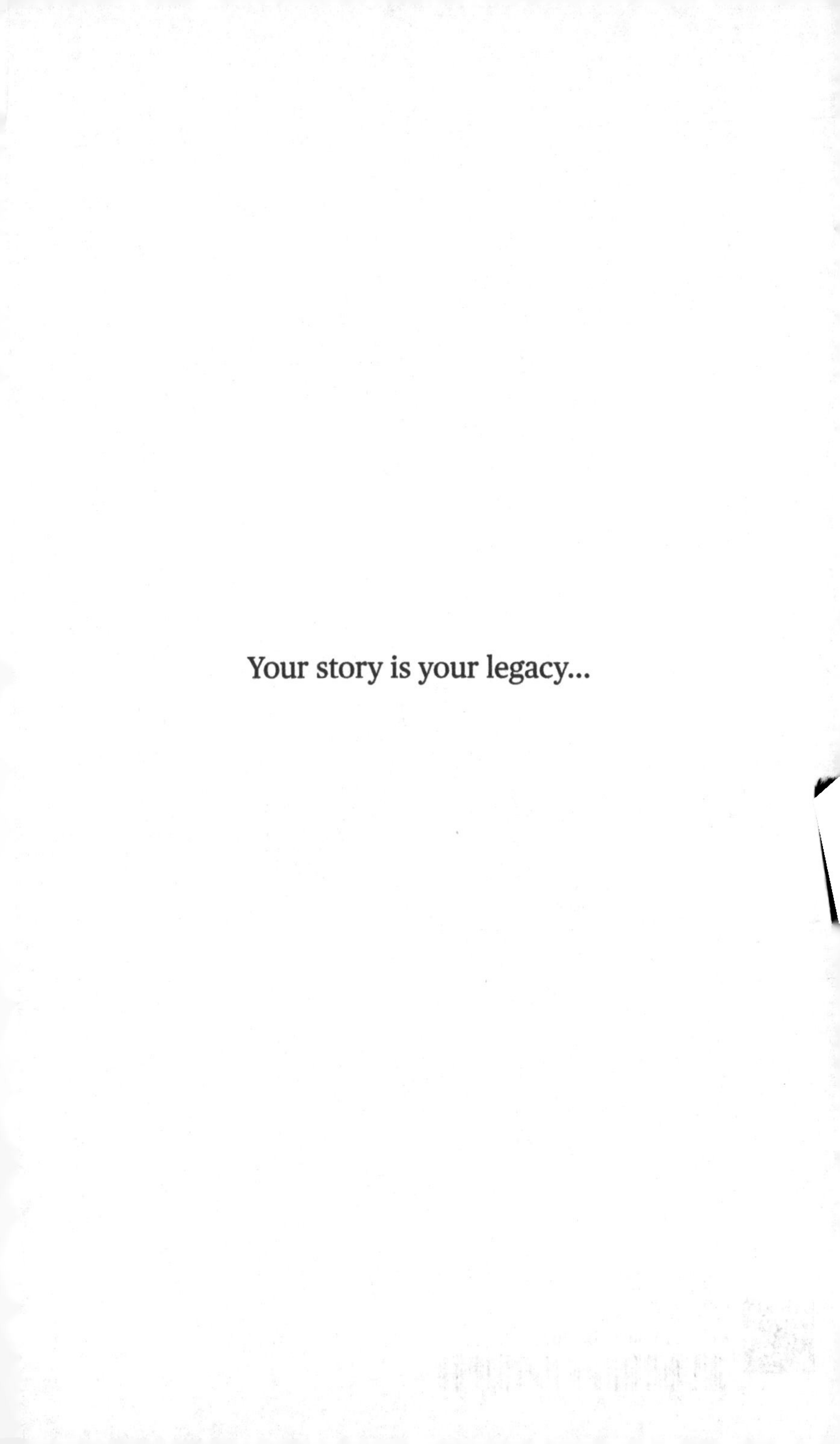

Your story is your legacy...

www.ingramcontent.com/pod-product-compliance
Lightning Source LLC
La Vergne TN
LVHW040221110826
845146LV00005B/1367

* 9 7 9 8 9 8 7 8 9 5 6 2 7 *